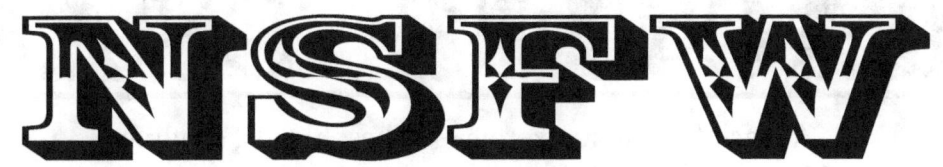

NSFW

(Not Safe For Work)

Calming Coloring of Adult Acronyms & Wayward Wordplay

by Damon Steele

TABLE OF CONTENTS

(In order of appearance)

I0390603

✦ *ISBN-13: 978-1540836403* ✦ *ISBN-10: 1540836401* ✦

PRACTICE SPACE

A place for you to exercise strokes, blends, shading,
and how to avoid spilling wine on the page as you go along.

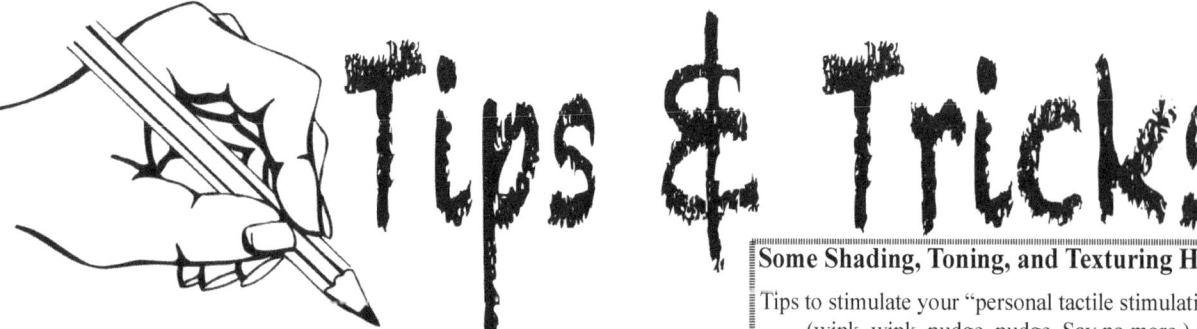

Tips & Tricks

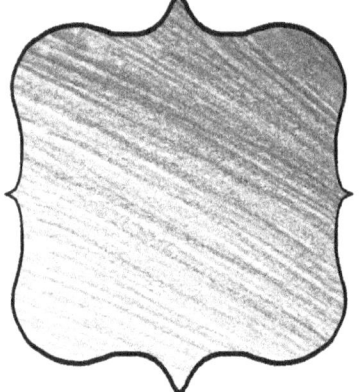

< Hatching

Hatching is created when parallel lines are used to indicate shading on or around an object. By changing the darkness of lines, and the amount of space between the lines, the artist can create a full range of value in the drawing. More space between the lines will lead to lighter values in the drawing. Less space between lines will lead to darker values in the shading.

Cross Hatching >

This technique is used to add further texture to shading by allowing the lines to cross over each other. The more frequently the lines intersect each other, the darker the value becomes. Your personal style will emerge when you practice this method frequently.

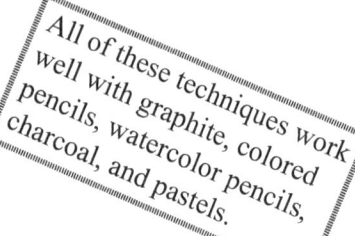

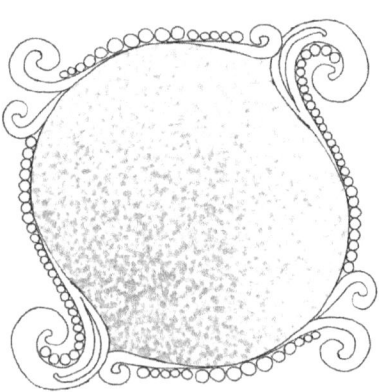

< Stippling

This method is created using dots to add texture, shadows, and tone. Much like hatching, the dots are denser where darkness is required, and more sparse, or lighter colored, to indicate highlights or a smooth surface. This technique can be used to create entire pieces of art simply from well placed dots.

All of these techniques work well with graphite, colored pencils, watercolor pencils, charcoal, and pastels.

Blending Stumps (Sticks) & Tortillons >

Our artsy ancient ancestors attained tone and depth using their fingers to blend and smudge charcoal or other pigments together. Once tired of messy fingerprints, they invented blending sticks as a less sloppy method. In modern times, blending stumps are compressed cylinders of paper sharpened to a point at each end. Tortillons have only one end that is sharp. Both come in a variety of widths, but the tips are equally sharp. Stumps can be tossed away when they become too dirty to use. However, rubbing the end against fine sandpaper will clean them. Think of it as a really fine pencil sharpener for your new best friend.

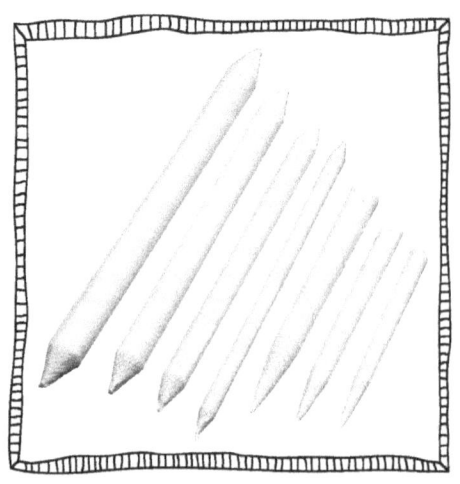

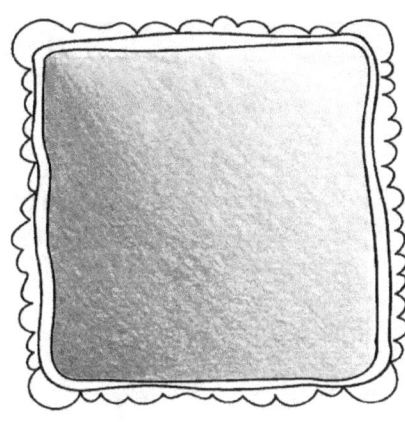

< Smudging

Use this texture technique to achieve finer gradients in shade and tone, to give your image greater depth and mood. Create your basic shading using broad strokes, denser and darker where the shadows deepen. Use your finger or a blending stump to smudge or smear the shading. The smudging will blur the tinting, making it smoother and more subtle.

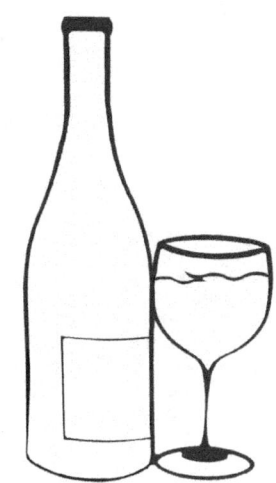

Random Color Hint:

This is a simple way to avoid an "Oops" moment.
~ Always apply your colors from light to dark. ~
It is easier to darken a color than it is to lighten it.

Burnishing >

This is achieved by applying heavy layers of color until the texture of the paper is filled in, thus a smooth, shiny surface is created. Burnished media has an almost painted appearance. Waxy pencils along with a blending stump may create a glossy transparent effect.

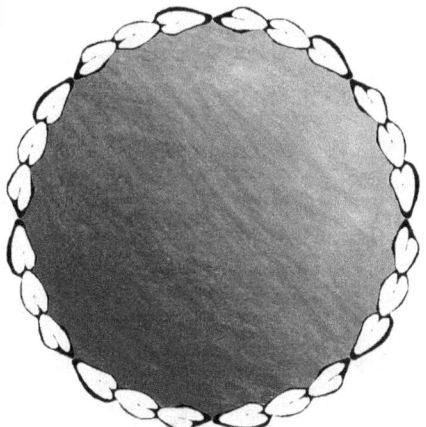

< Circular Scumbling

Using varied scribbles, or small circular strokes, drawn closer together and overlapping, the darker this will appear. When the scribbles or circular strokes are drawn further apart it creates a lighter effect. This technique can be a sharp effect as needed, or rubbed with a blending stump to achieve a softened texture.

3-D Shading >

This is a simplified tutorial, combining textures and tones to create a three-dimensional effect. This is not an exact stroke for stroke "How To Guide" rather a "Cliff Notes" version. All of these steps can be augmented by using texture techniques. Rule one for achieving dimensionality is to always work from light to dark. Start the portion to be highlighted by undercoating it in white, or the lightest color you want seen. Work your base color (halftone) into the areas not washed by the brightest light. Then, also add this color to the shadow areas. Add the darkest version of your color, or black, over the deepest shadow areas. Blend from the halftone into the highlight, then from the deepest shadows toward the halftone and reflection areas. Repeat this shading for cast shadows and your project will easily take on a satisfying shape.

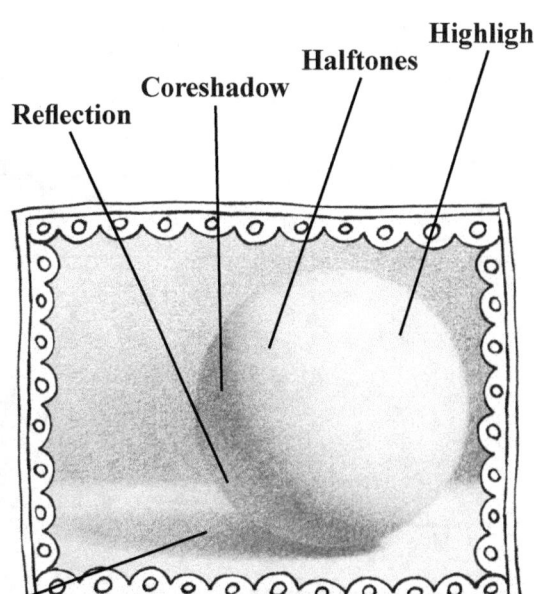

Reflection Coreshadow Halftones Highlight

Cast Shadow

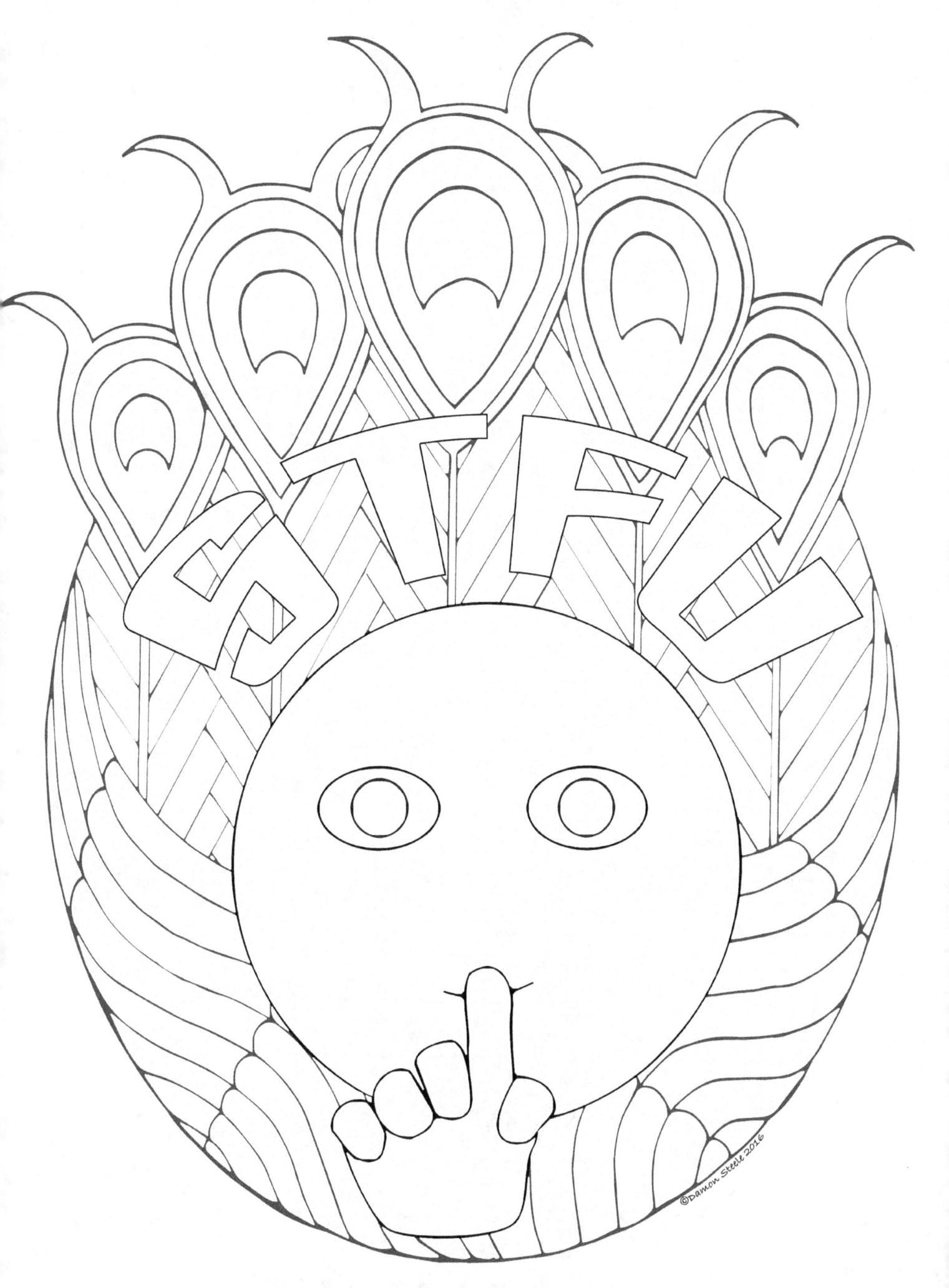

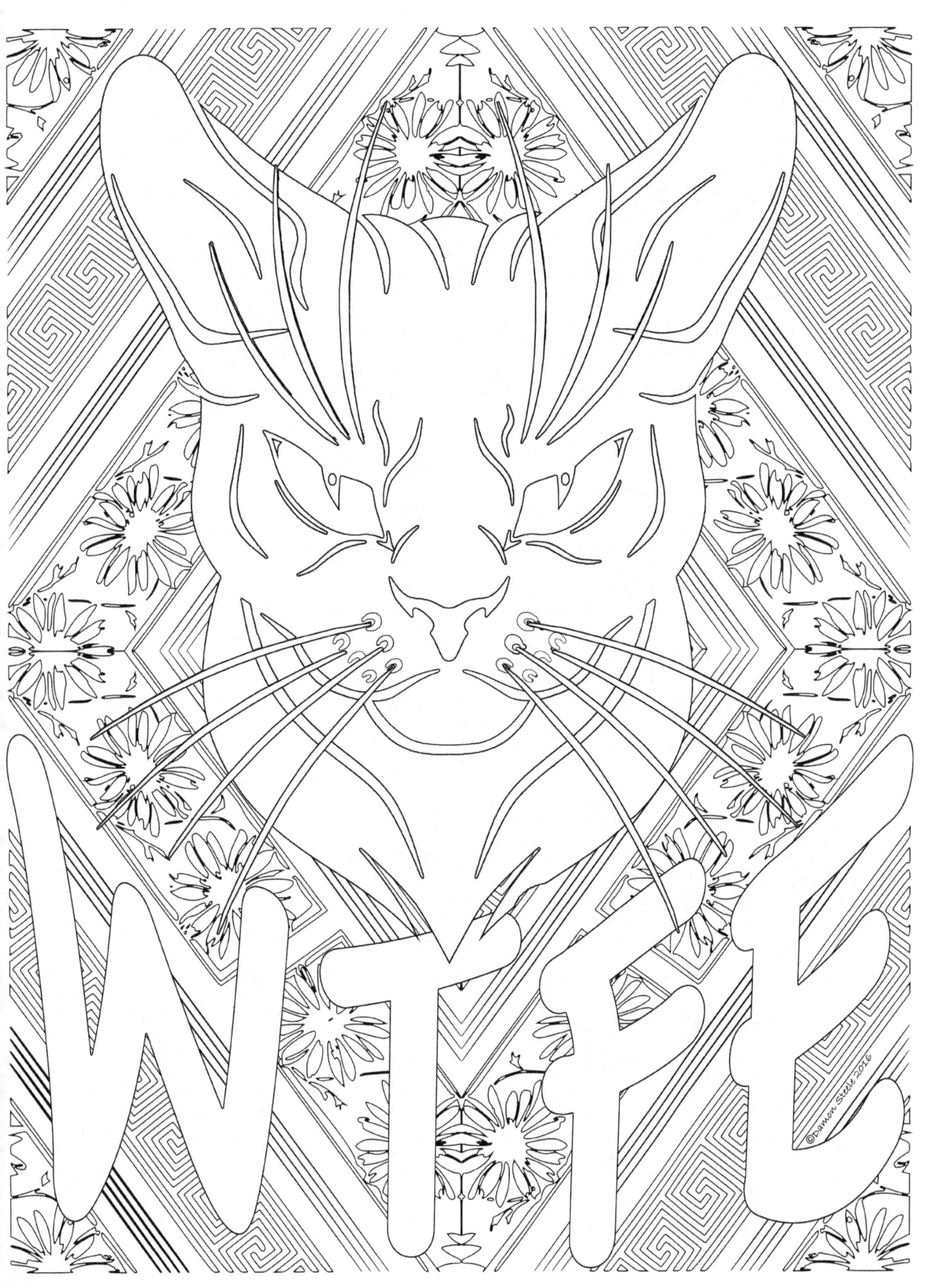

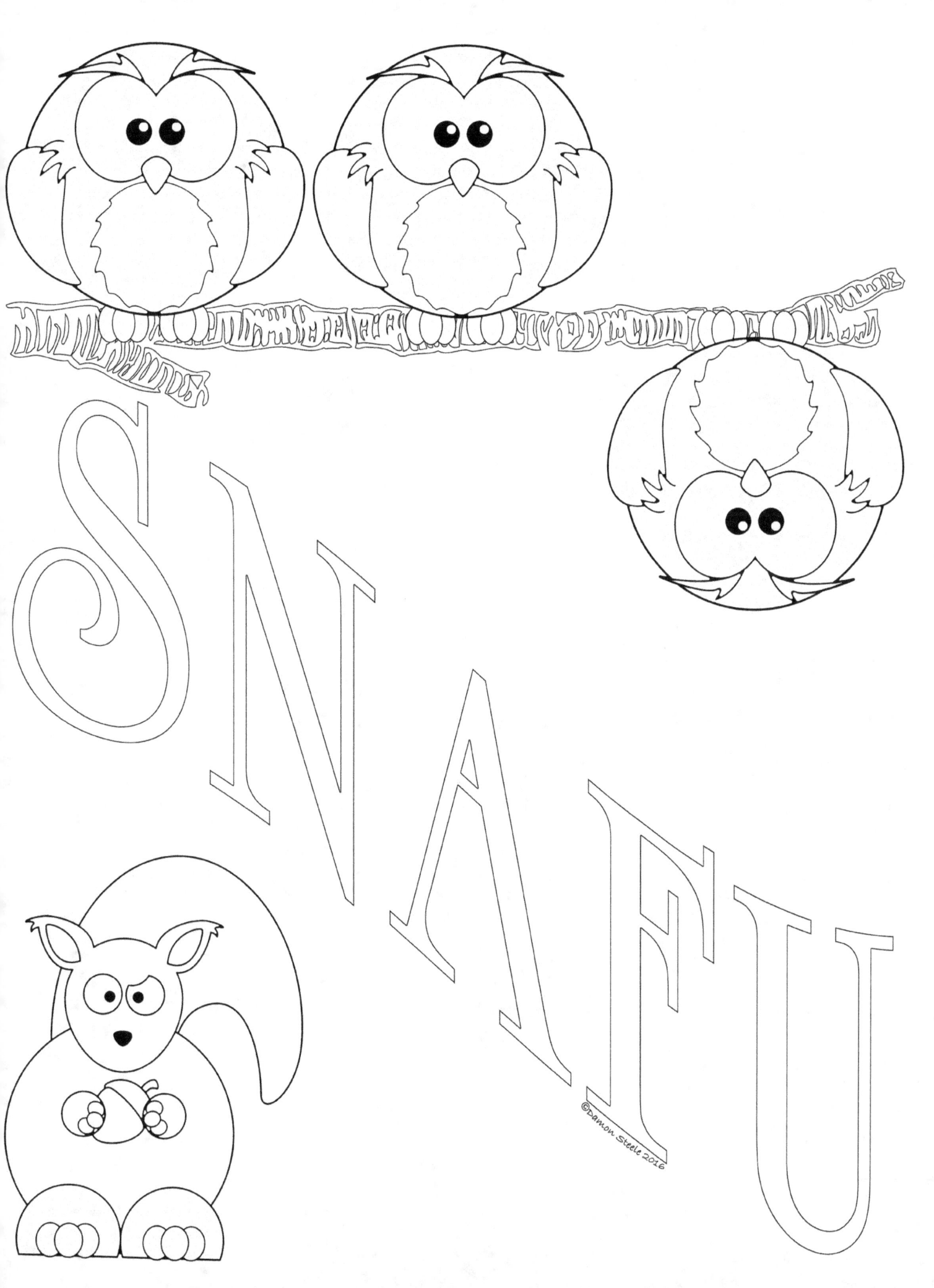

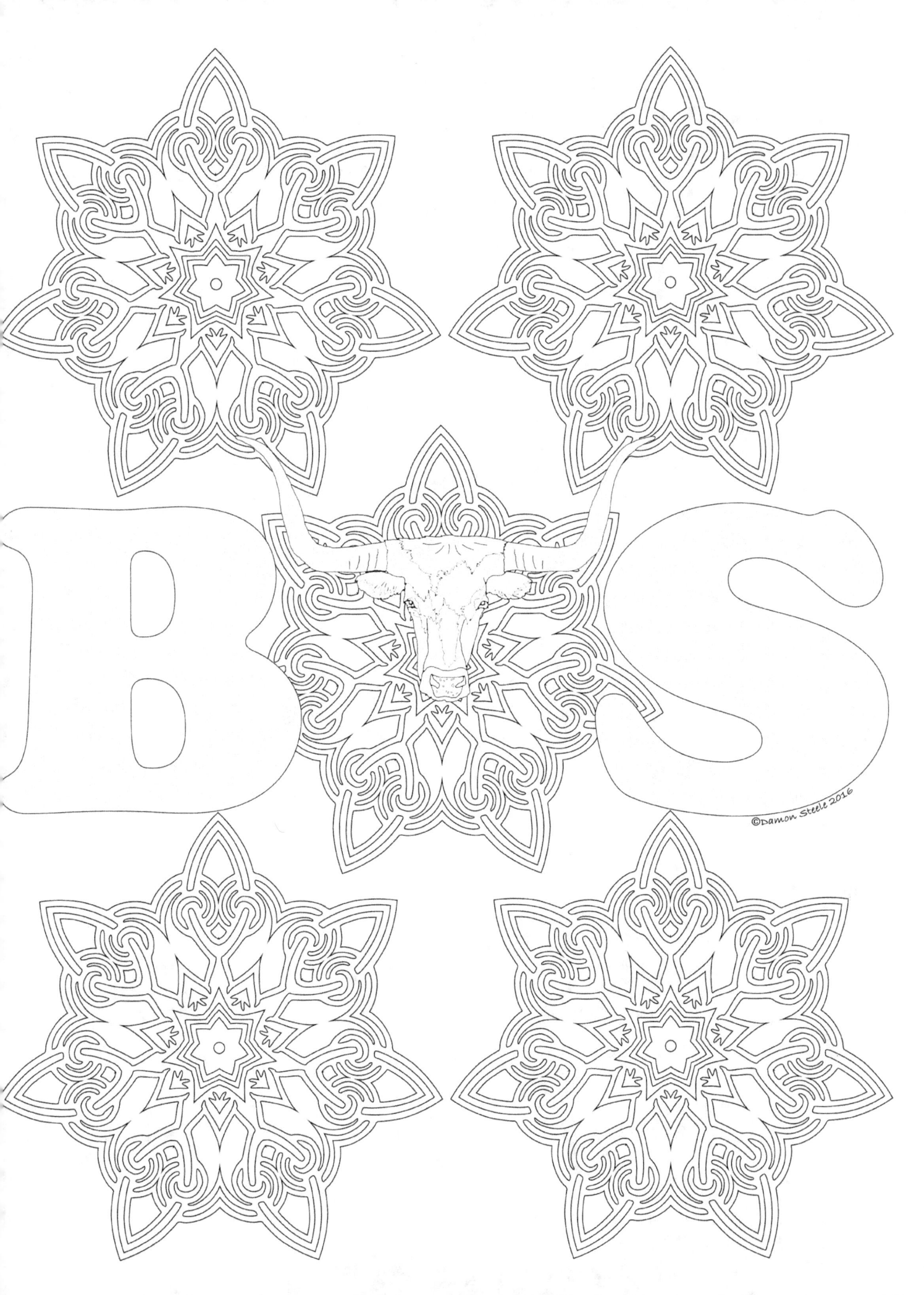

©Damon Steele 2016

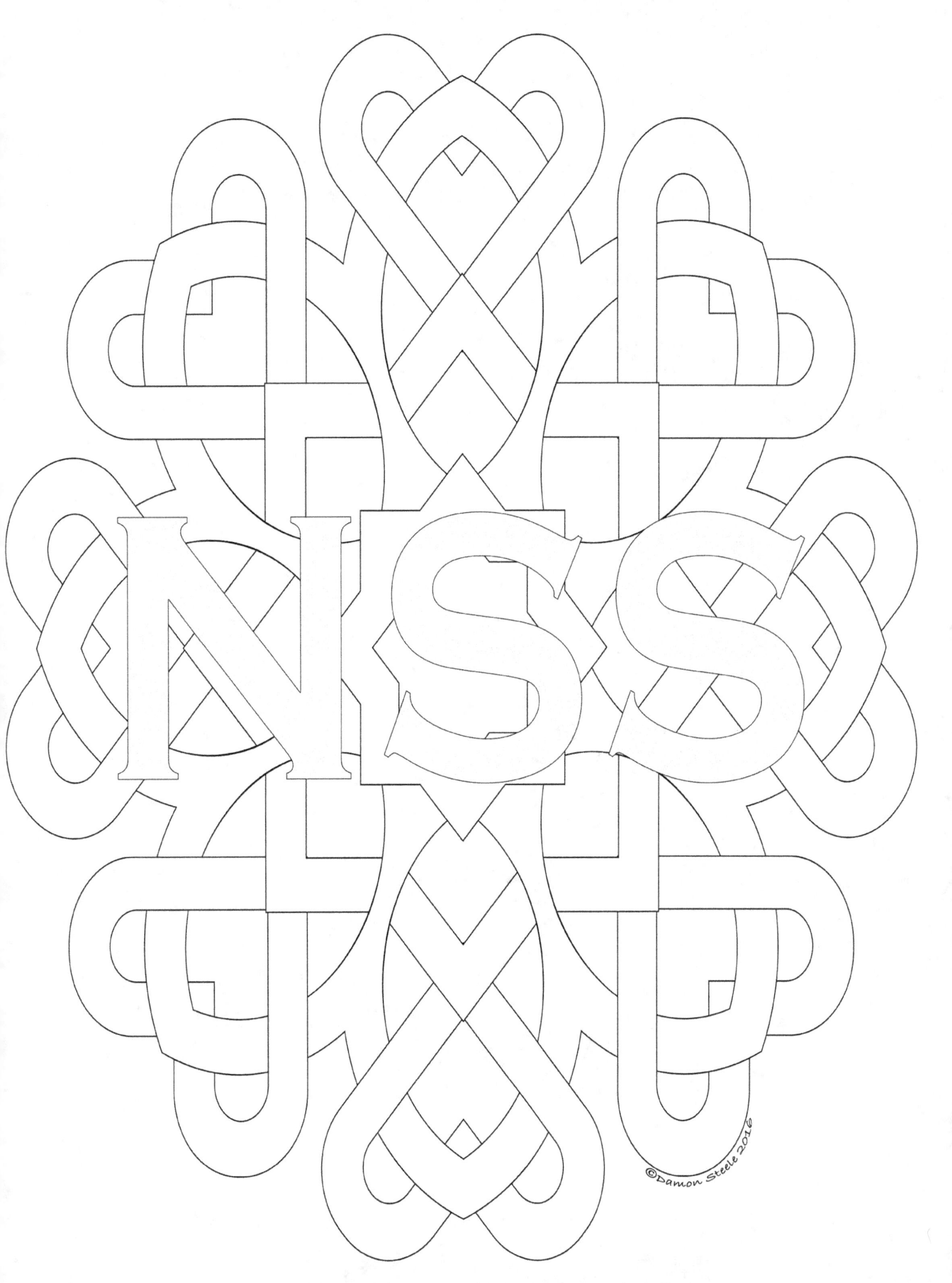

©Damon Steele 2016

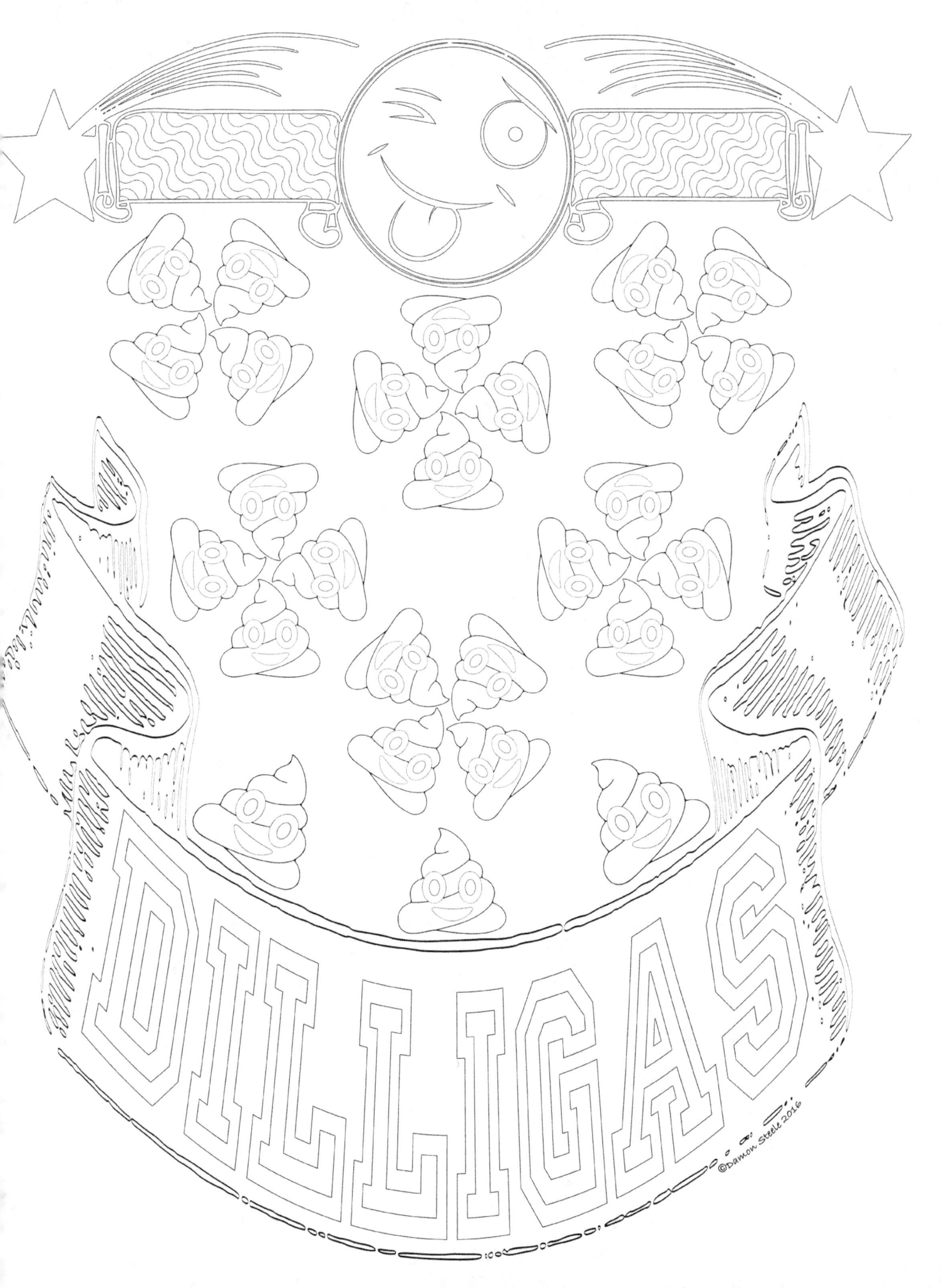

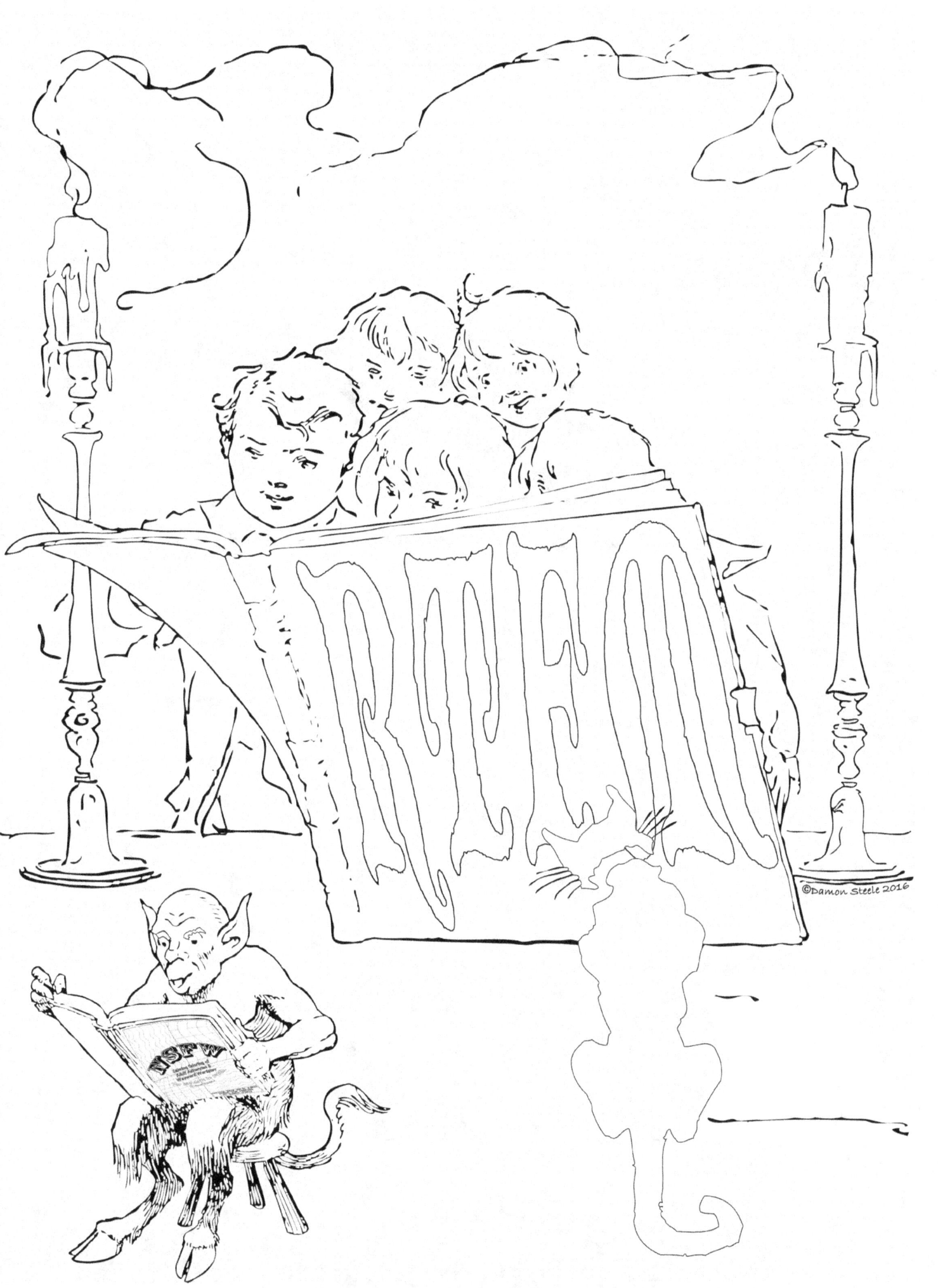

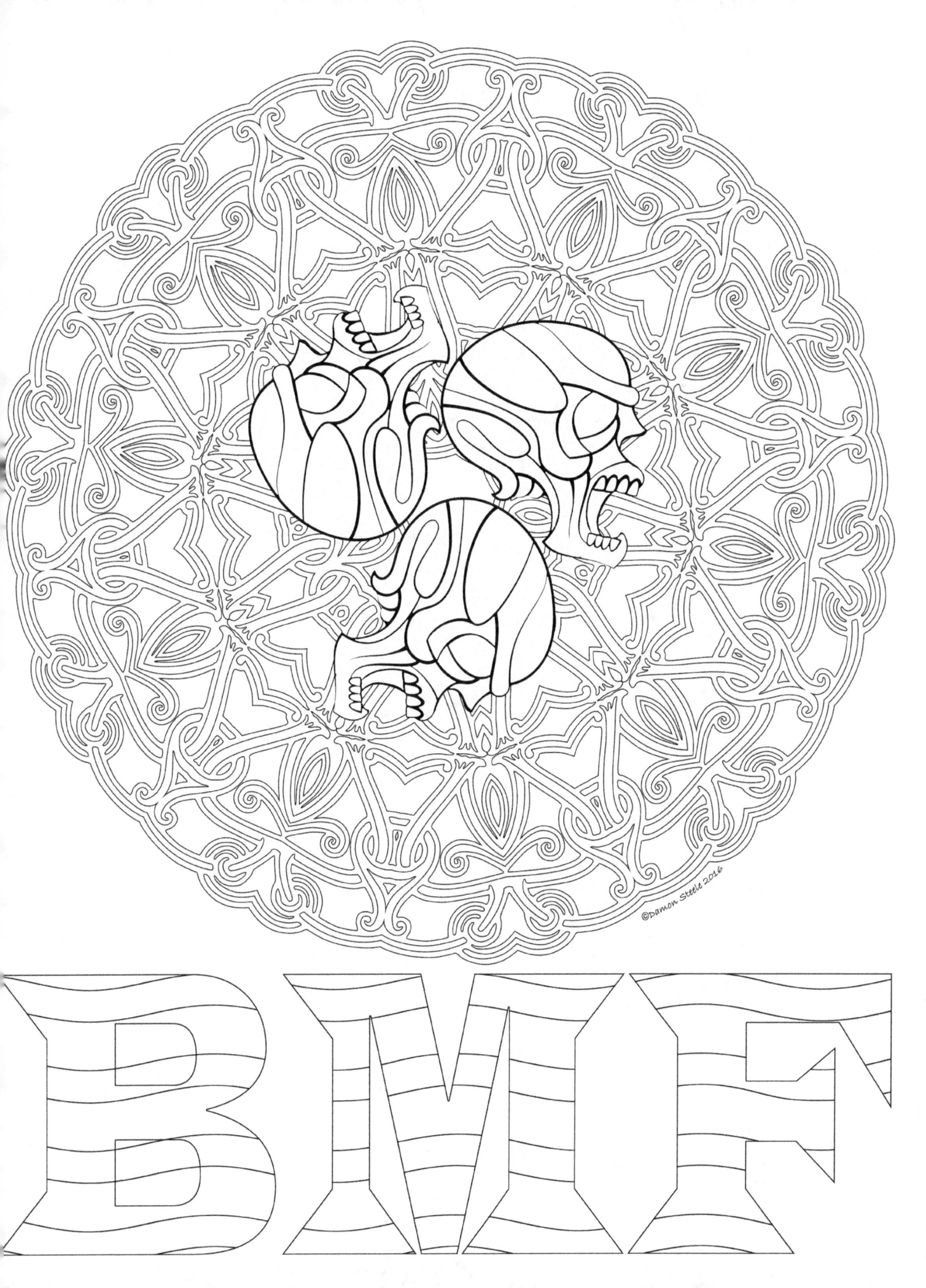

©Damon Steele 2016

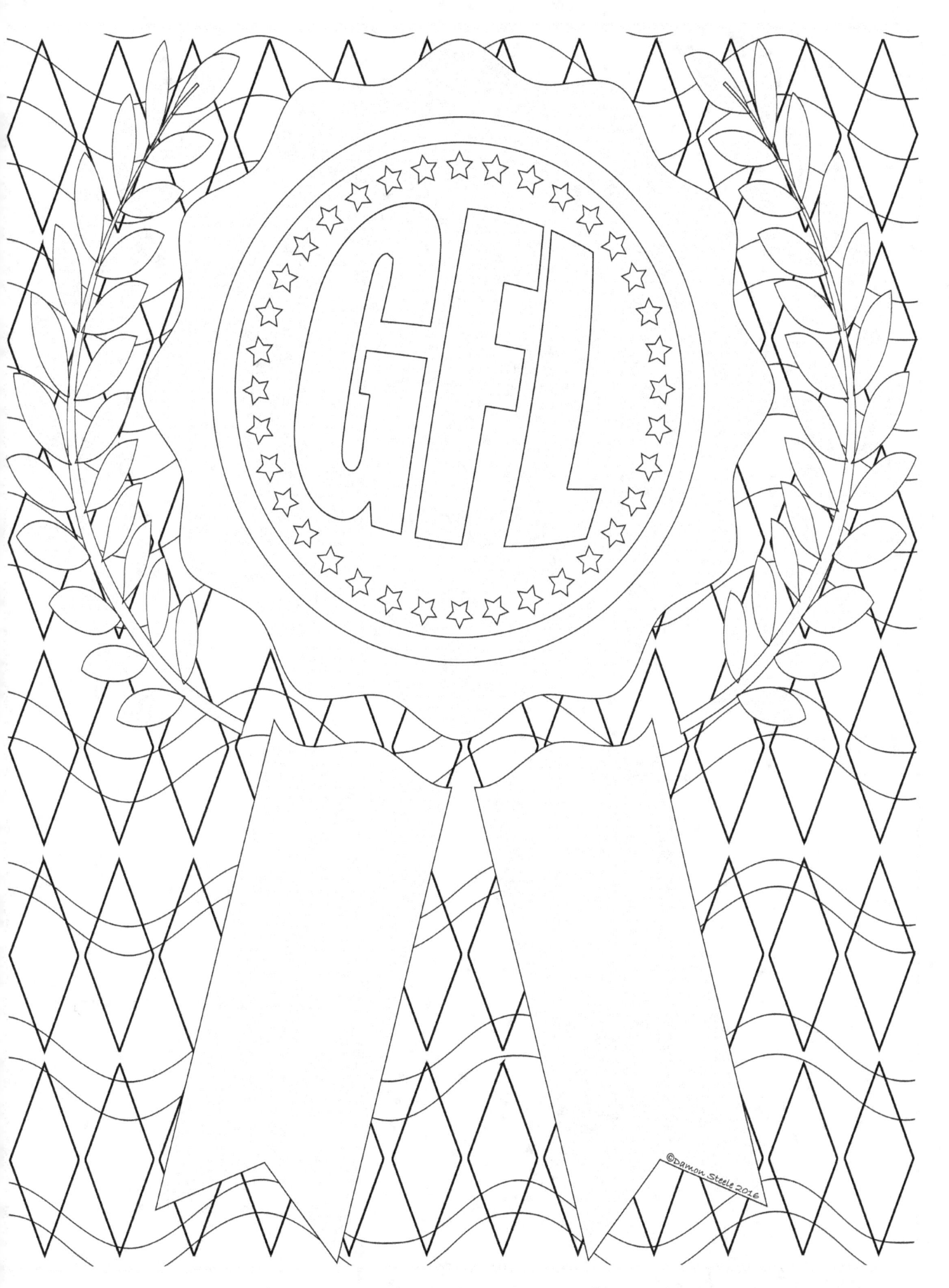

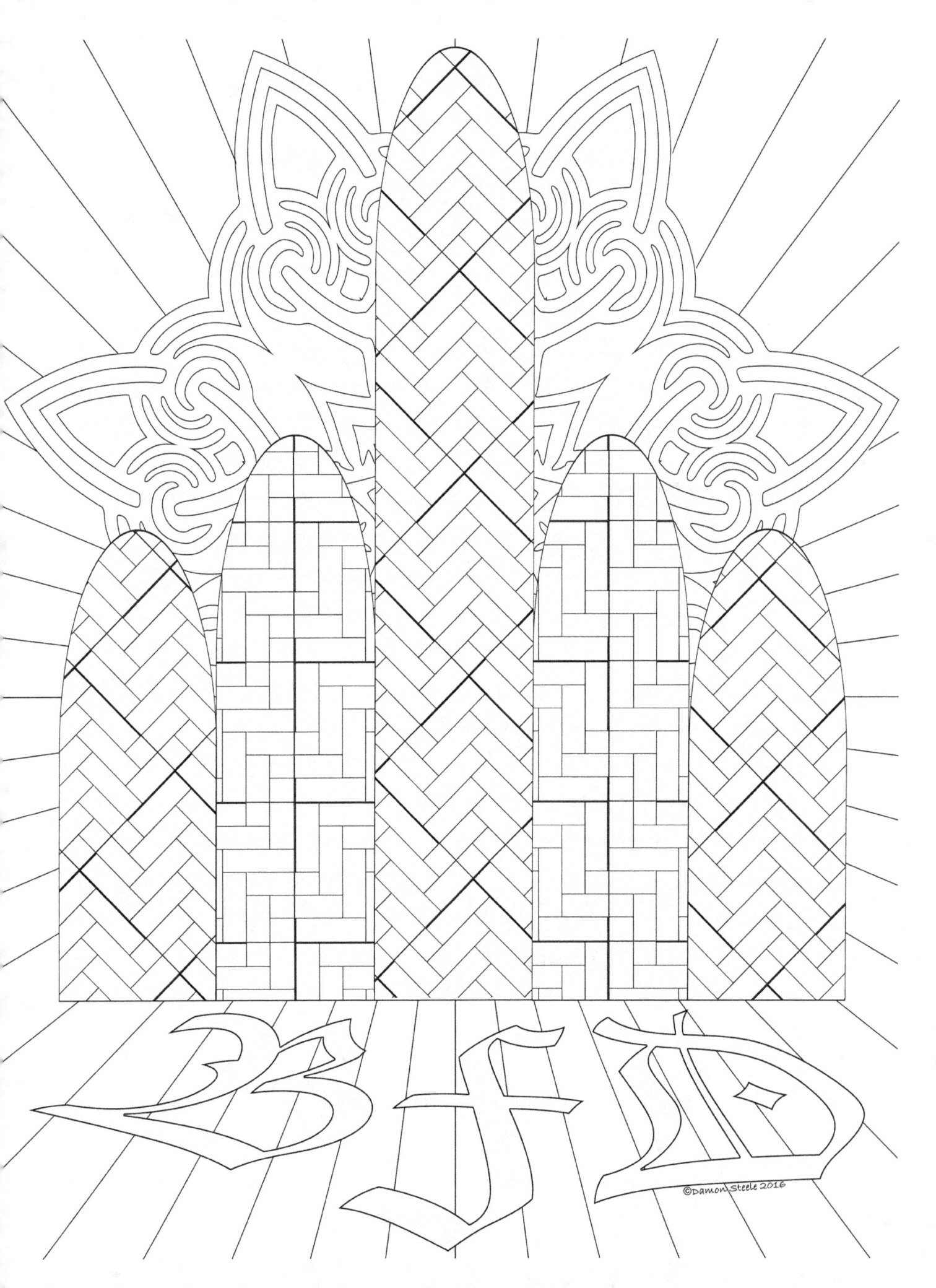

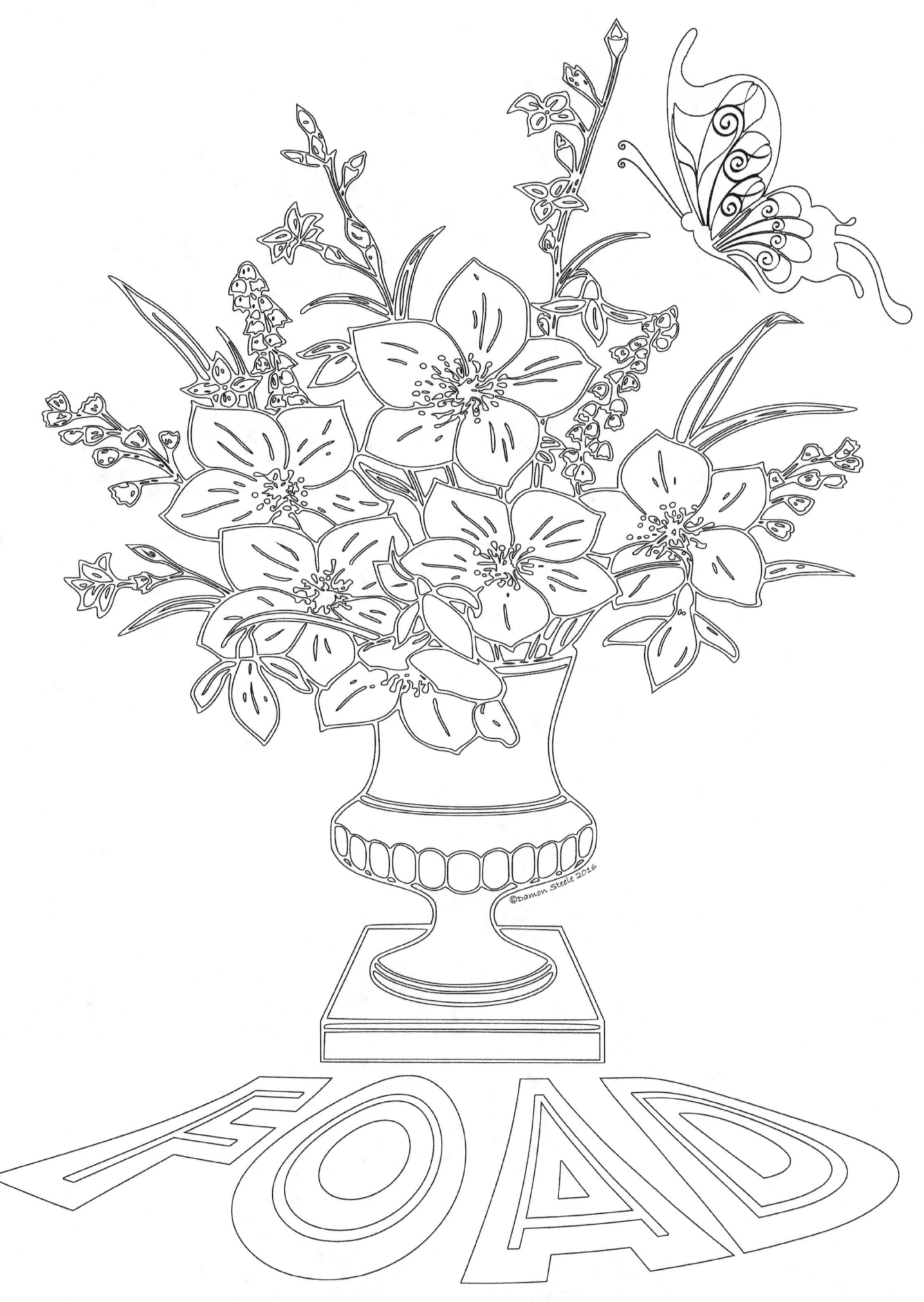

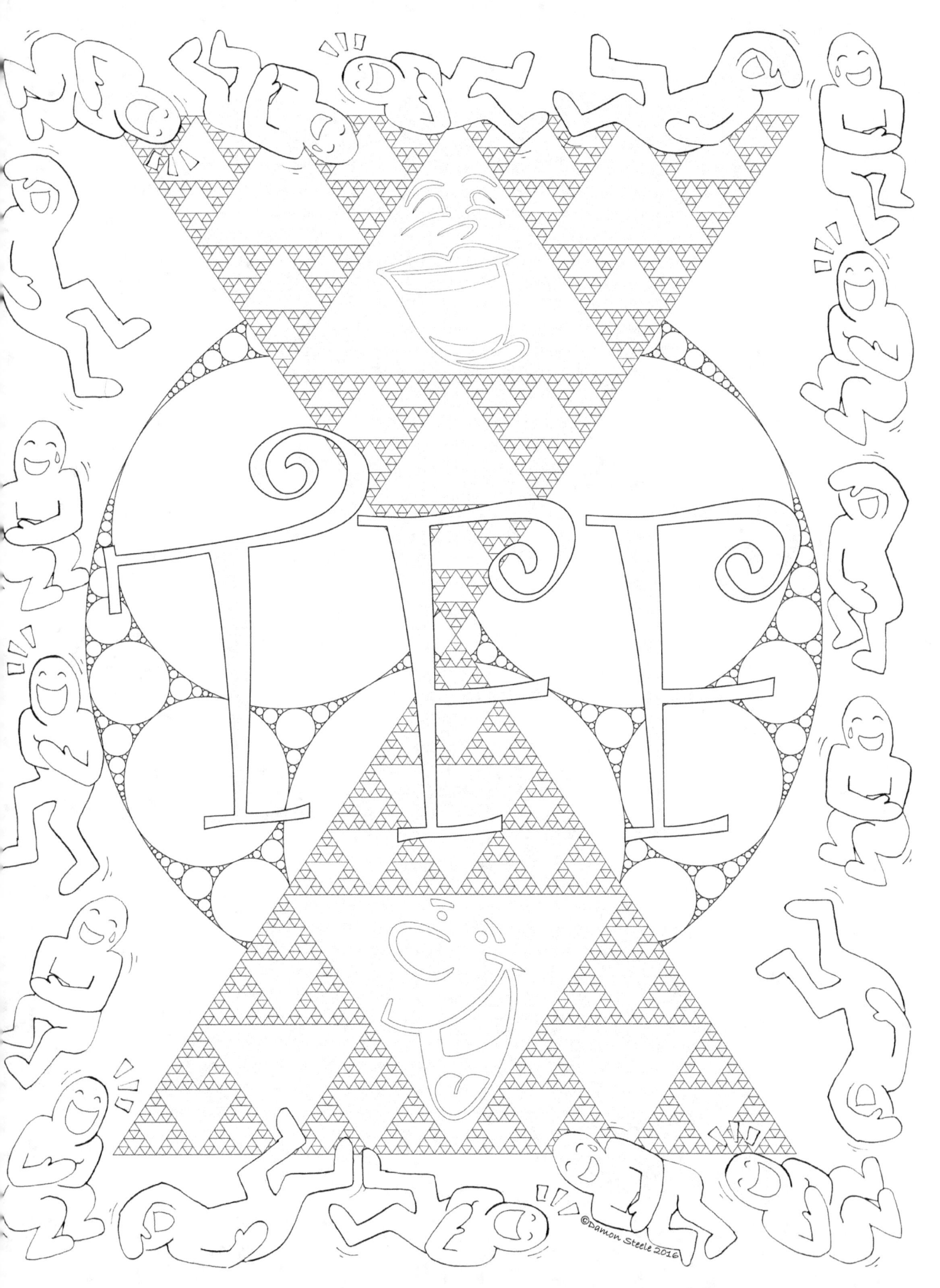

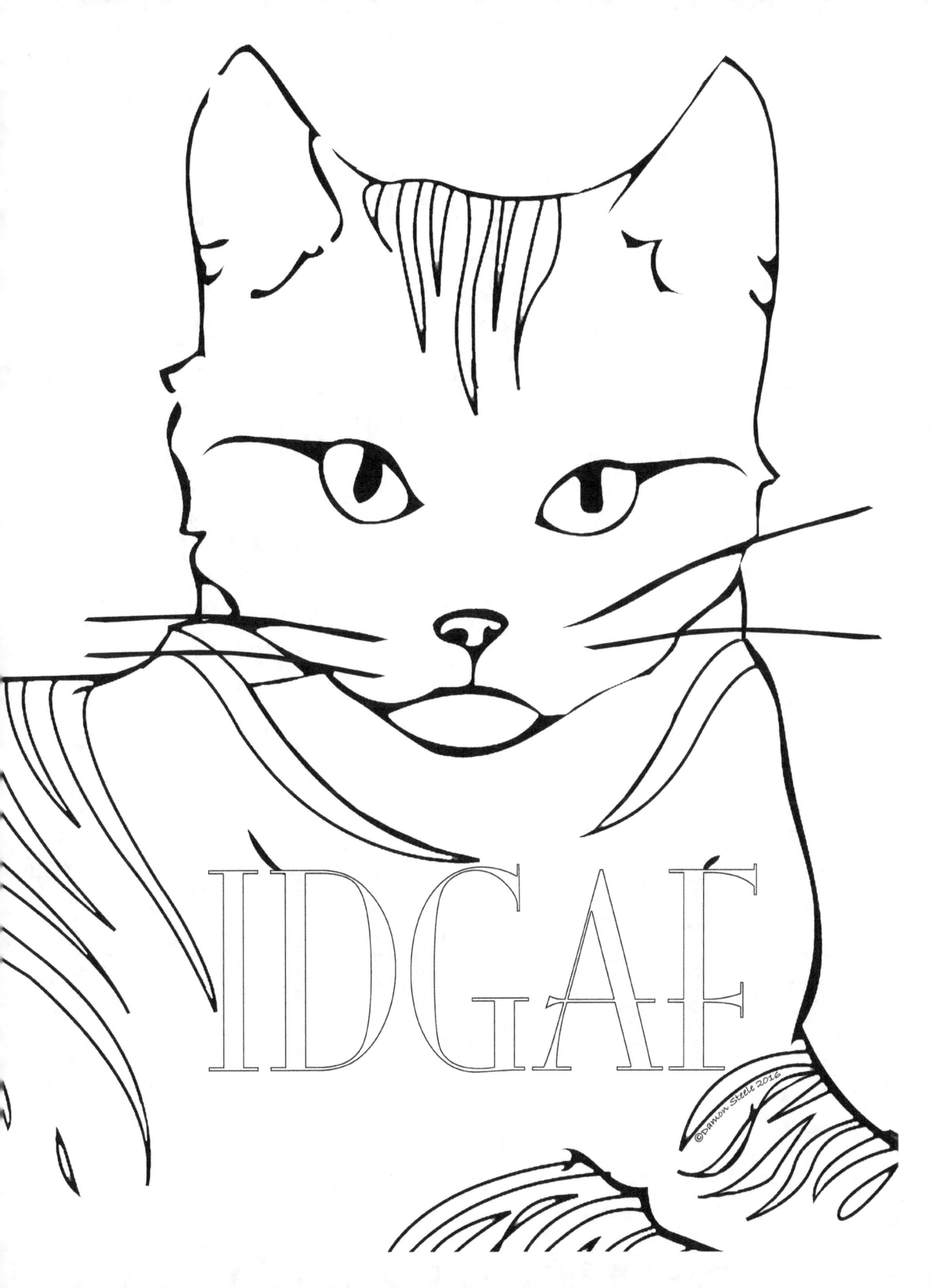

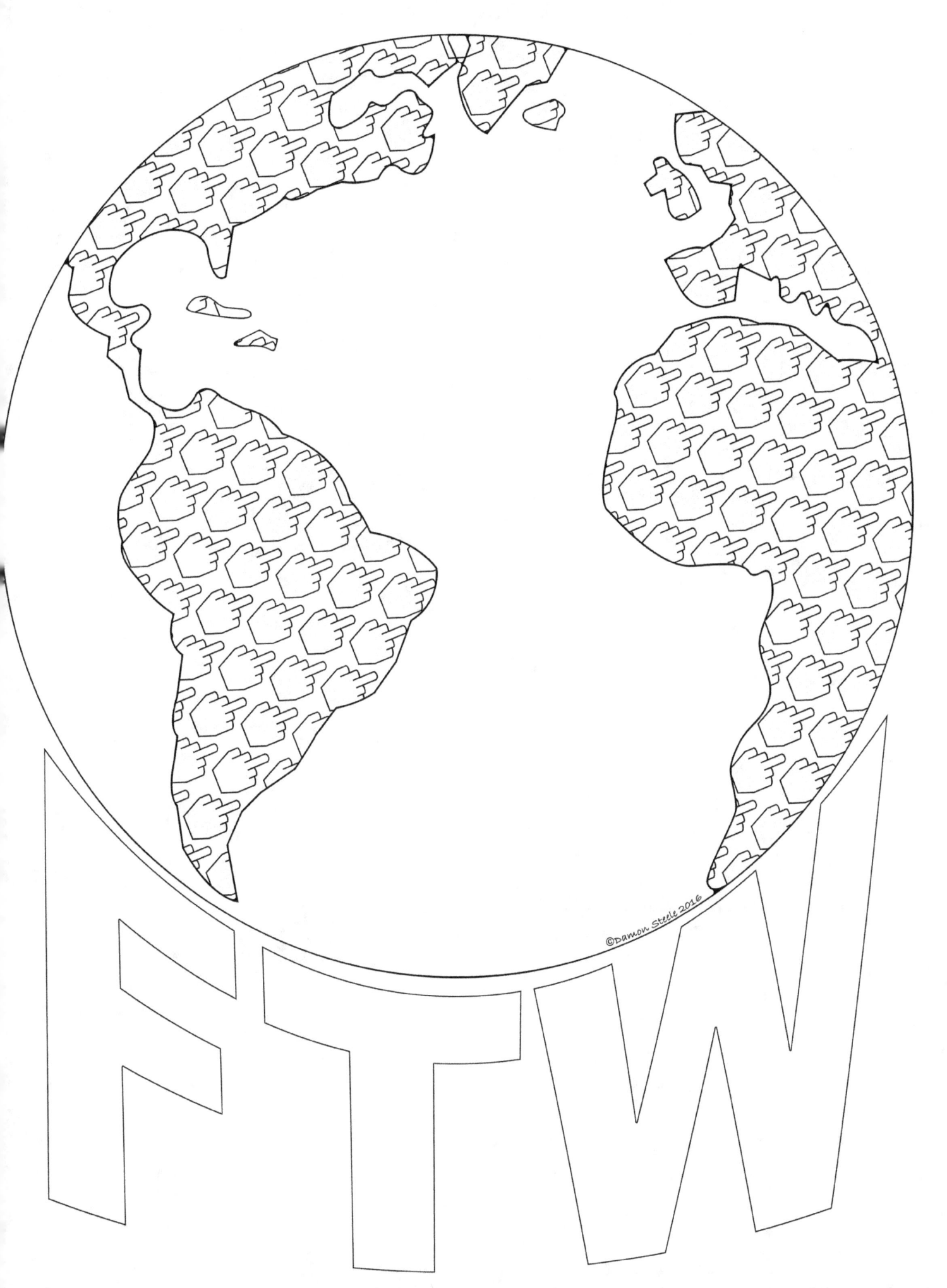

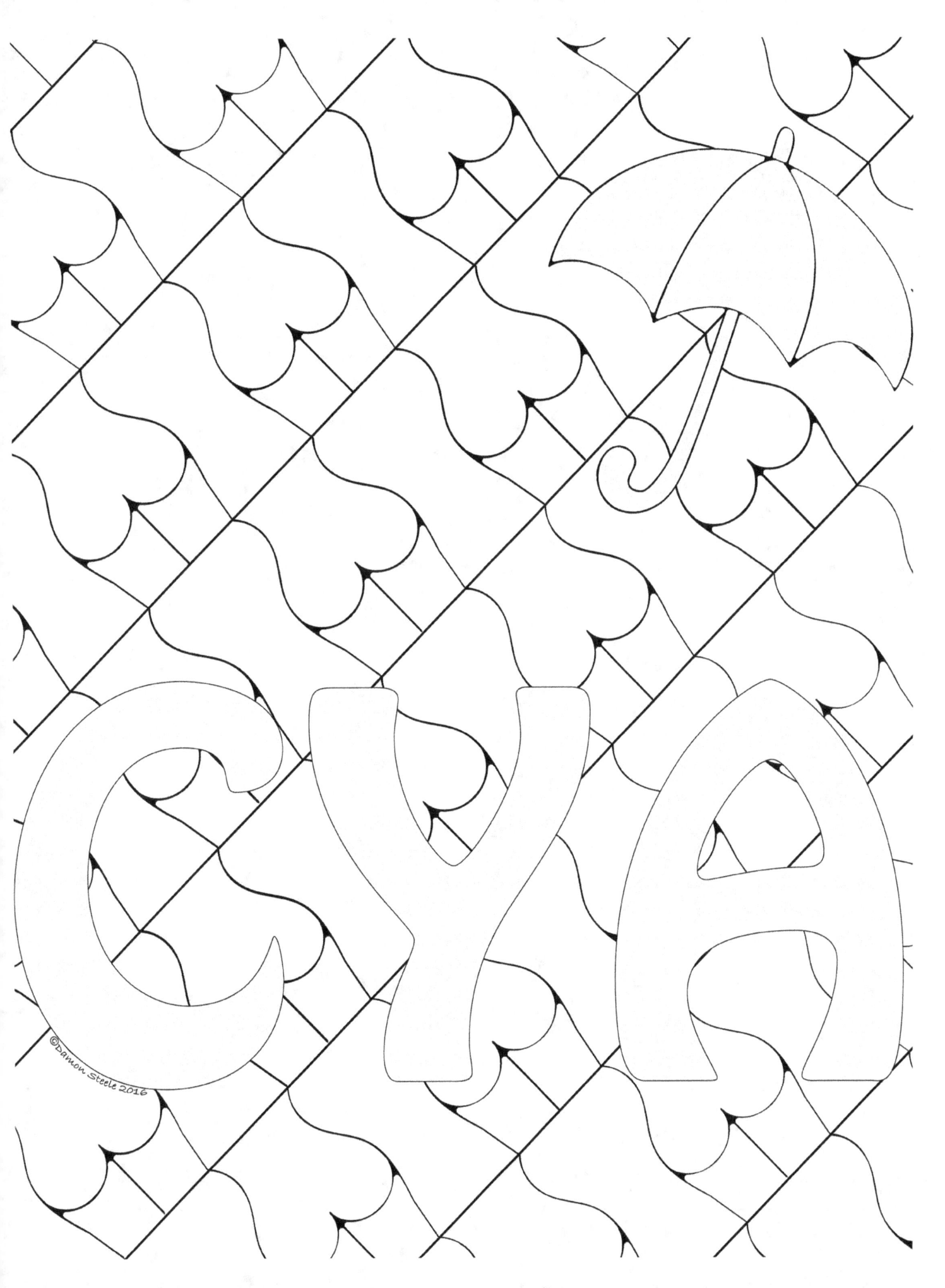
©Damon Steele 2016

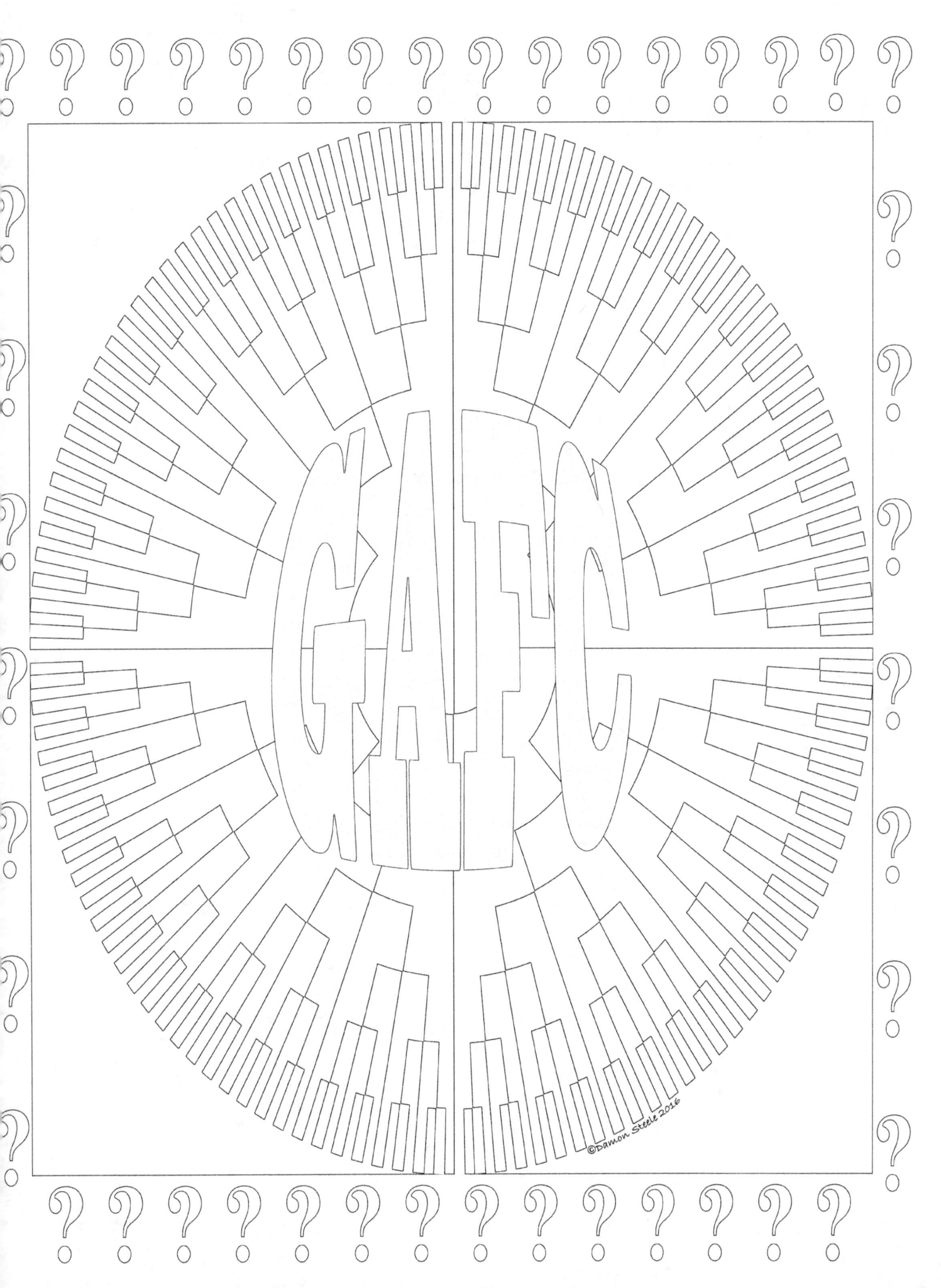

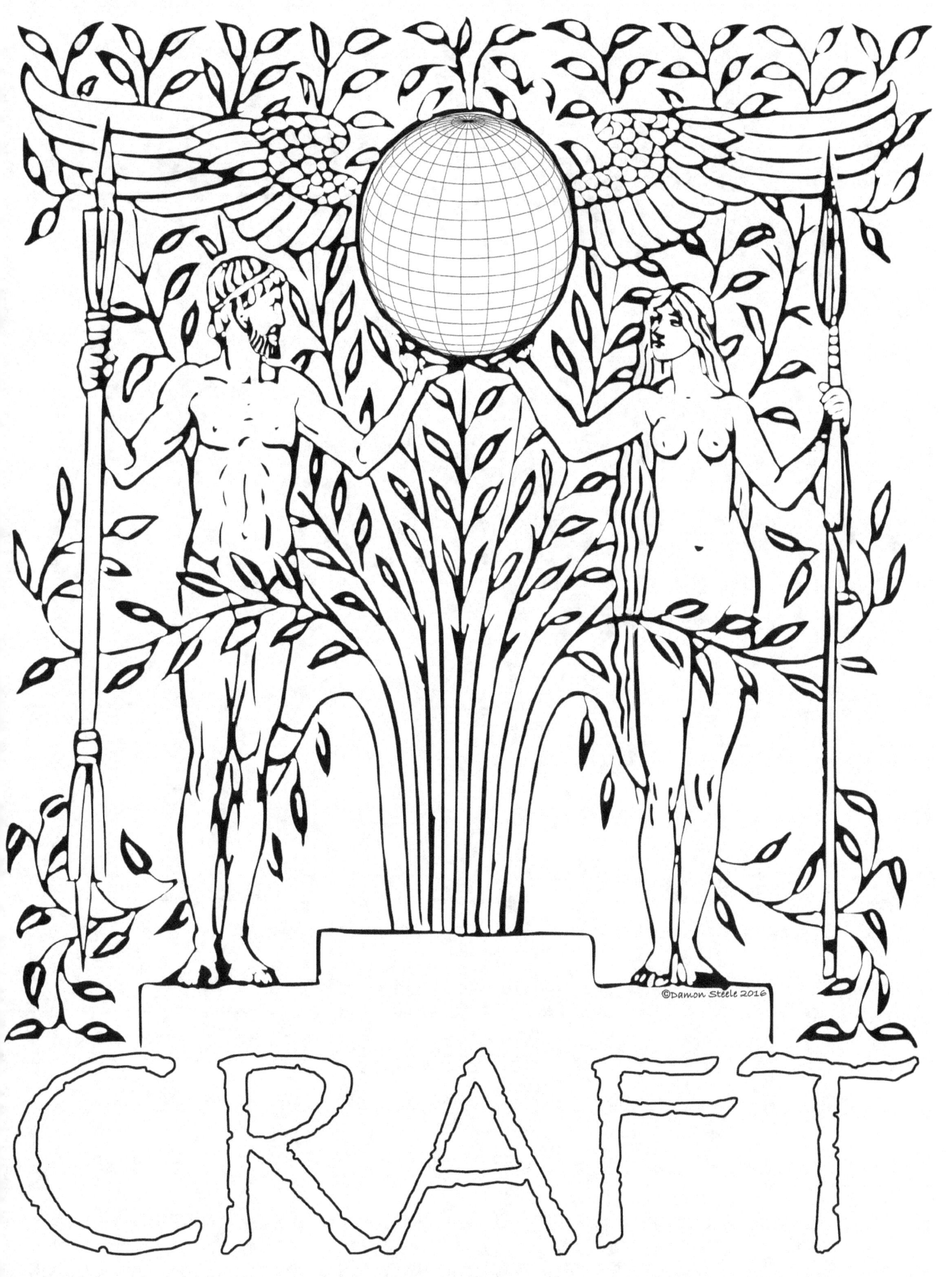

©Damon Steele 2016

CRAFT

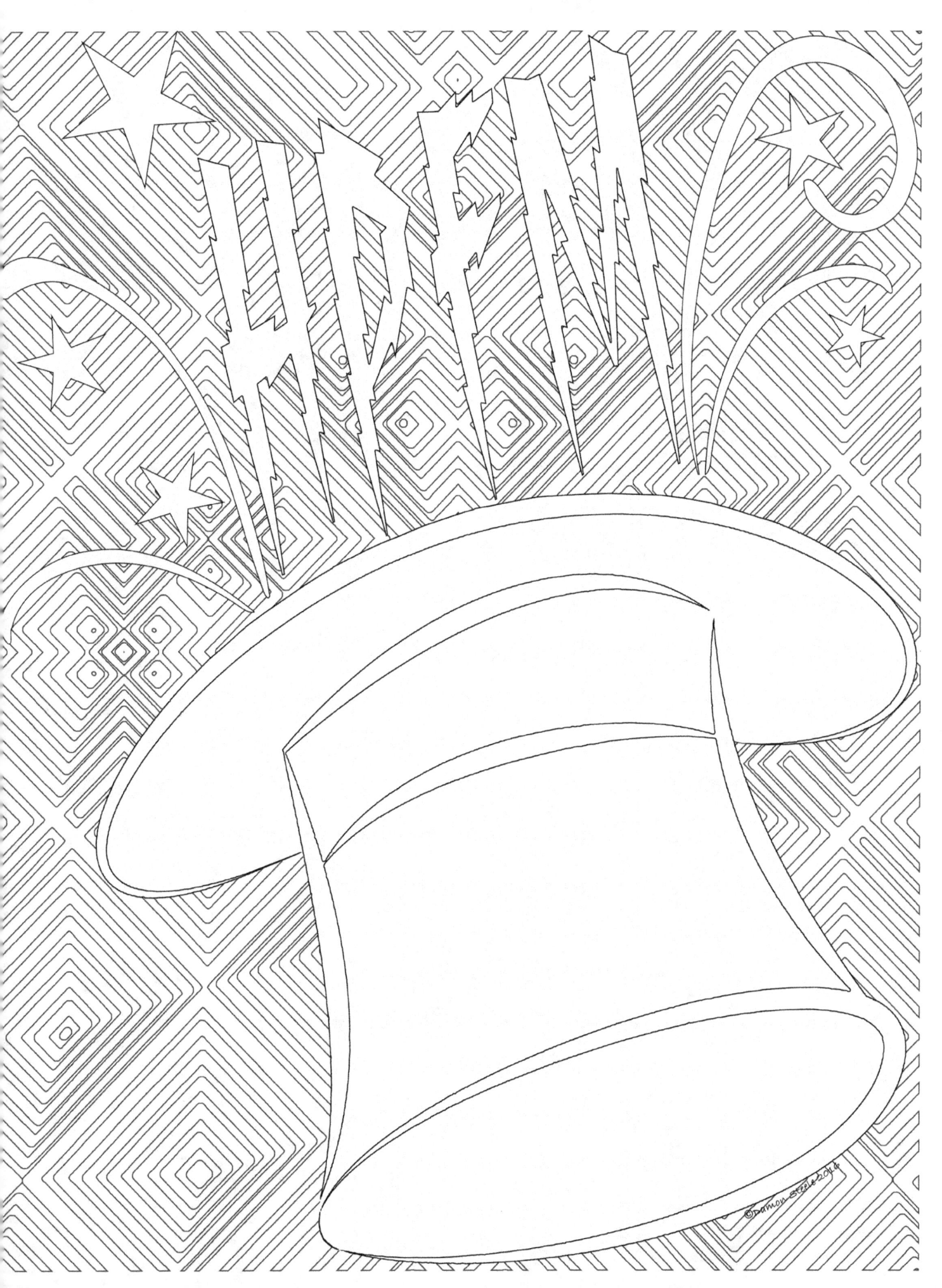

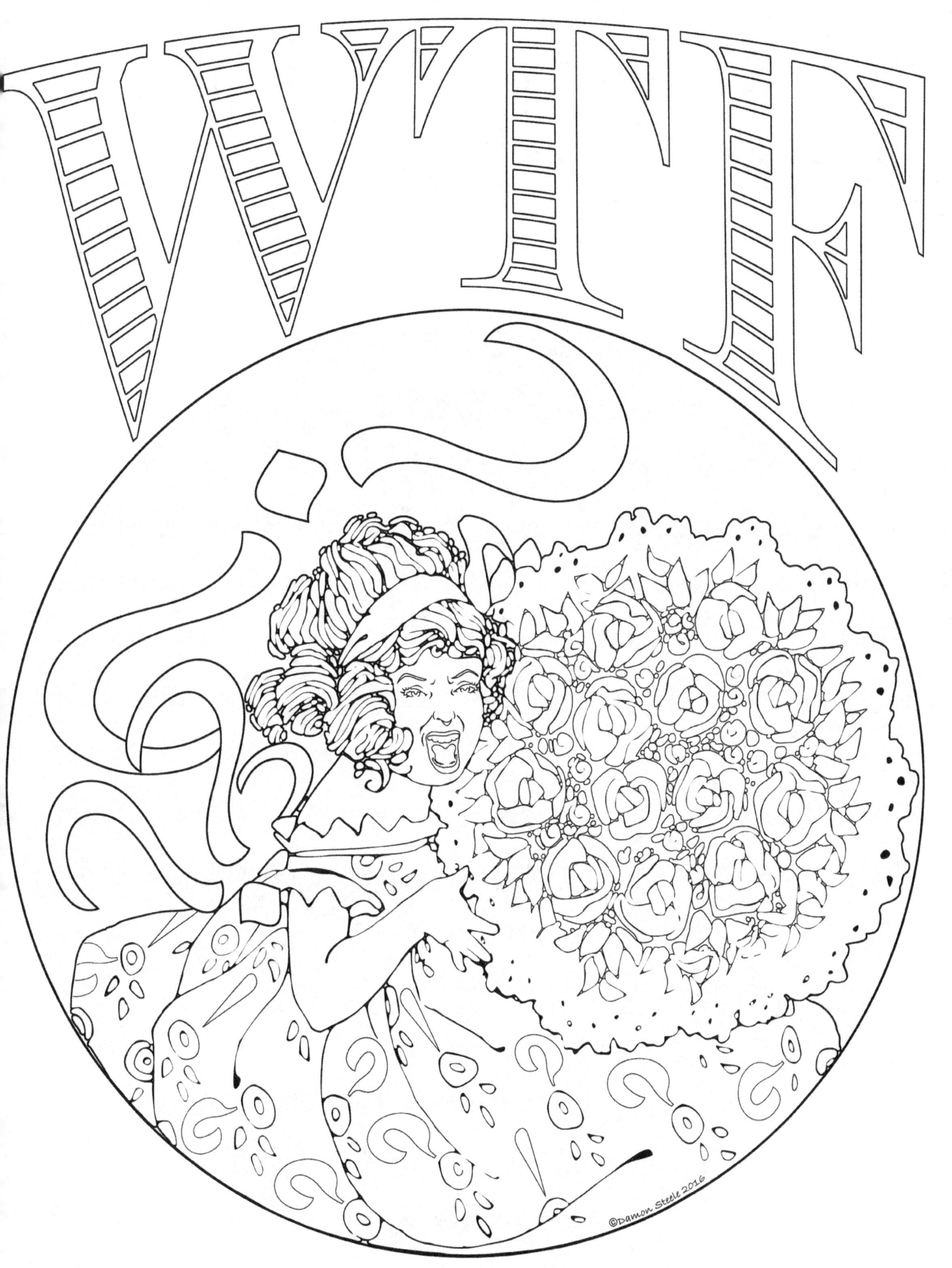

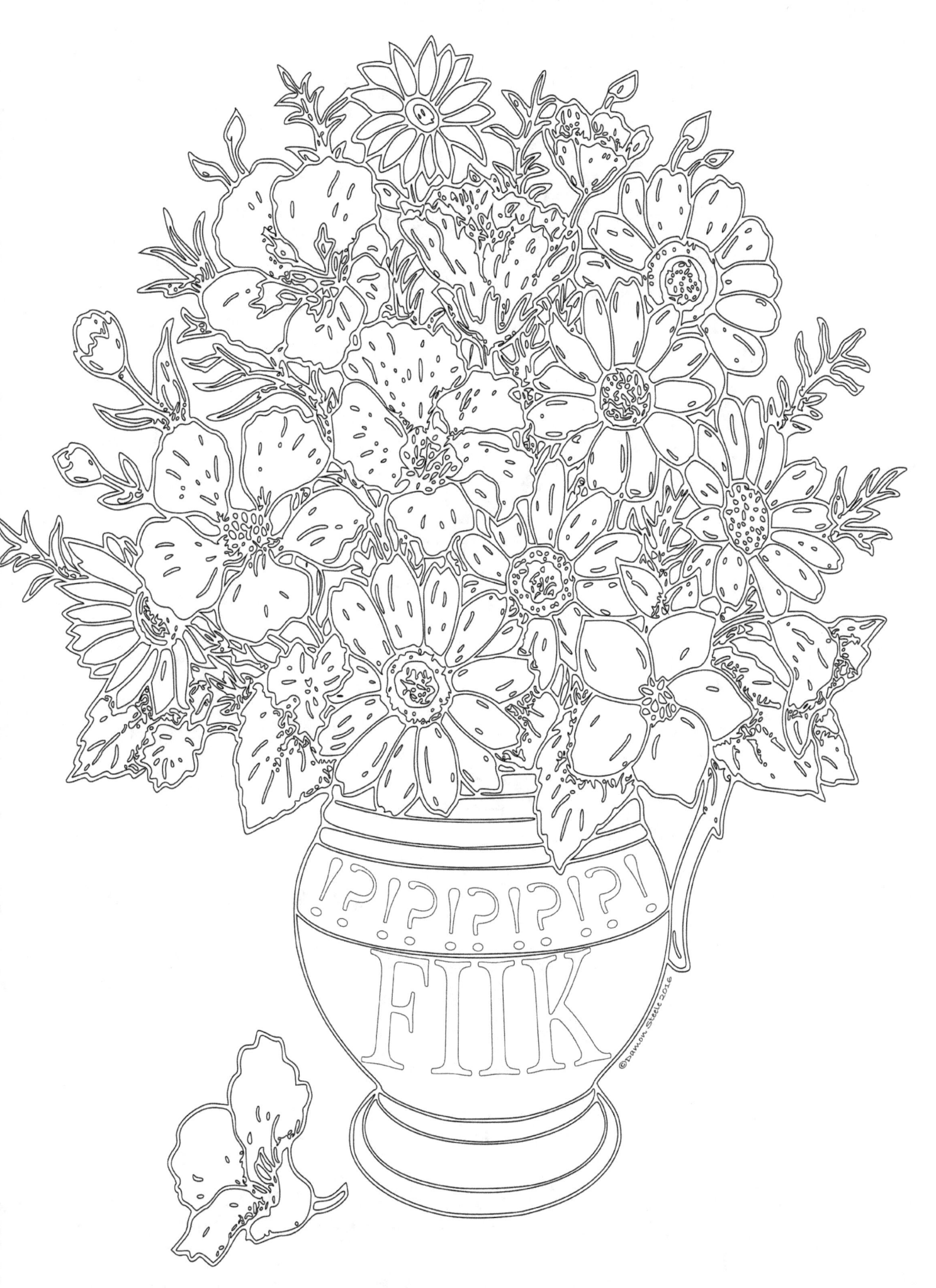

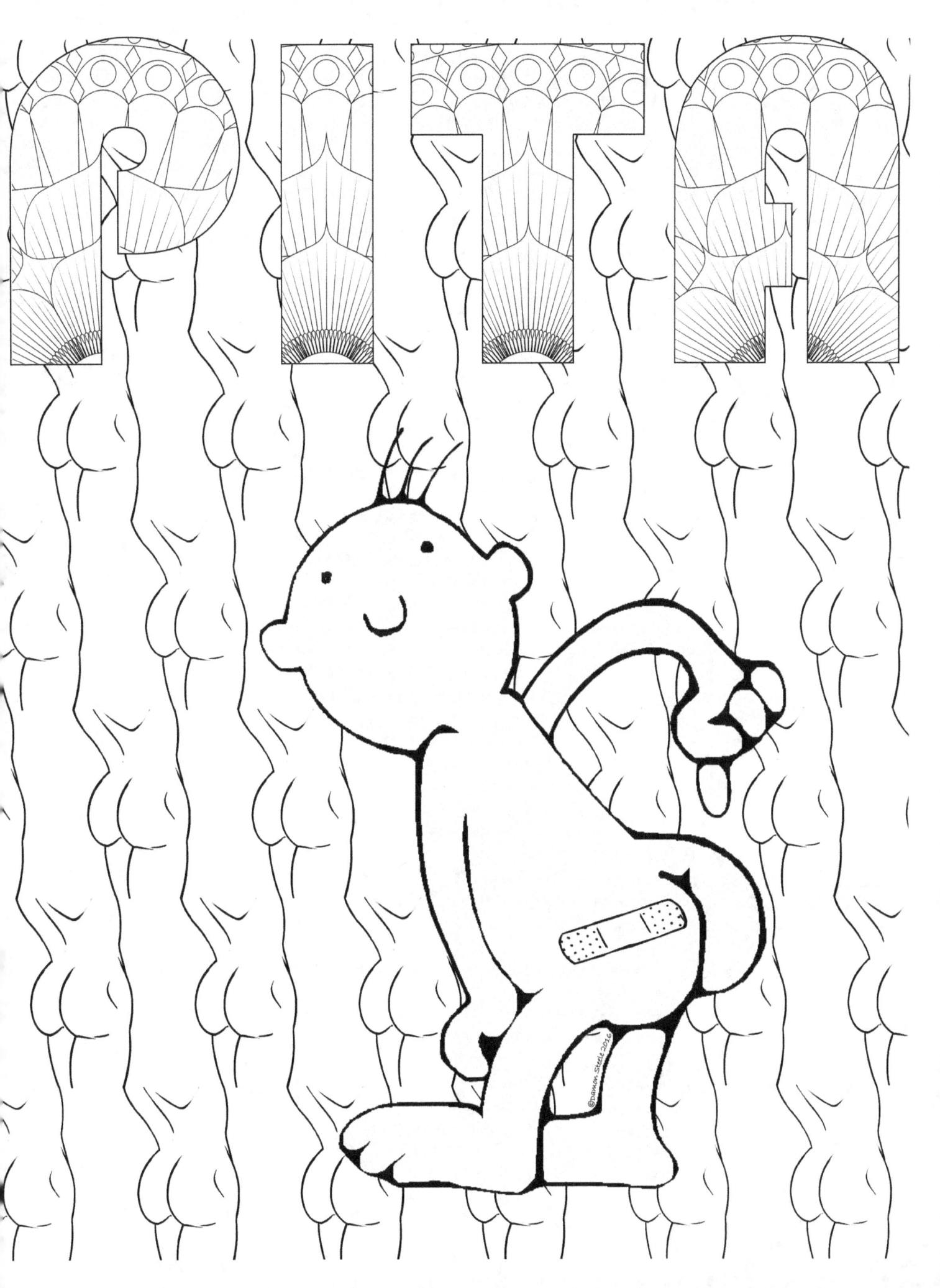

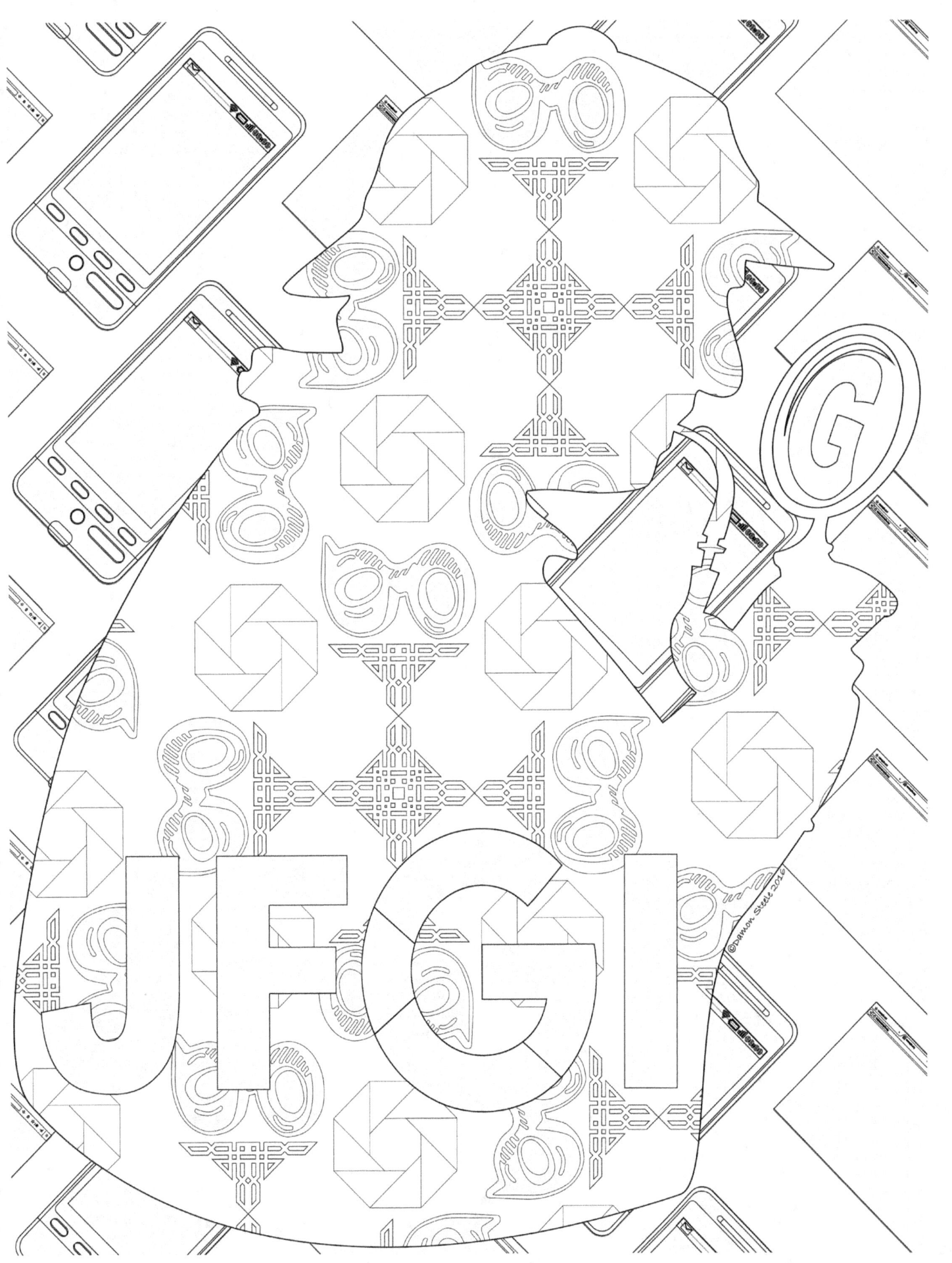

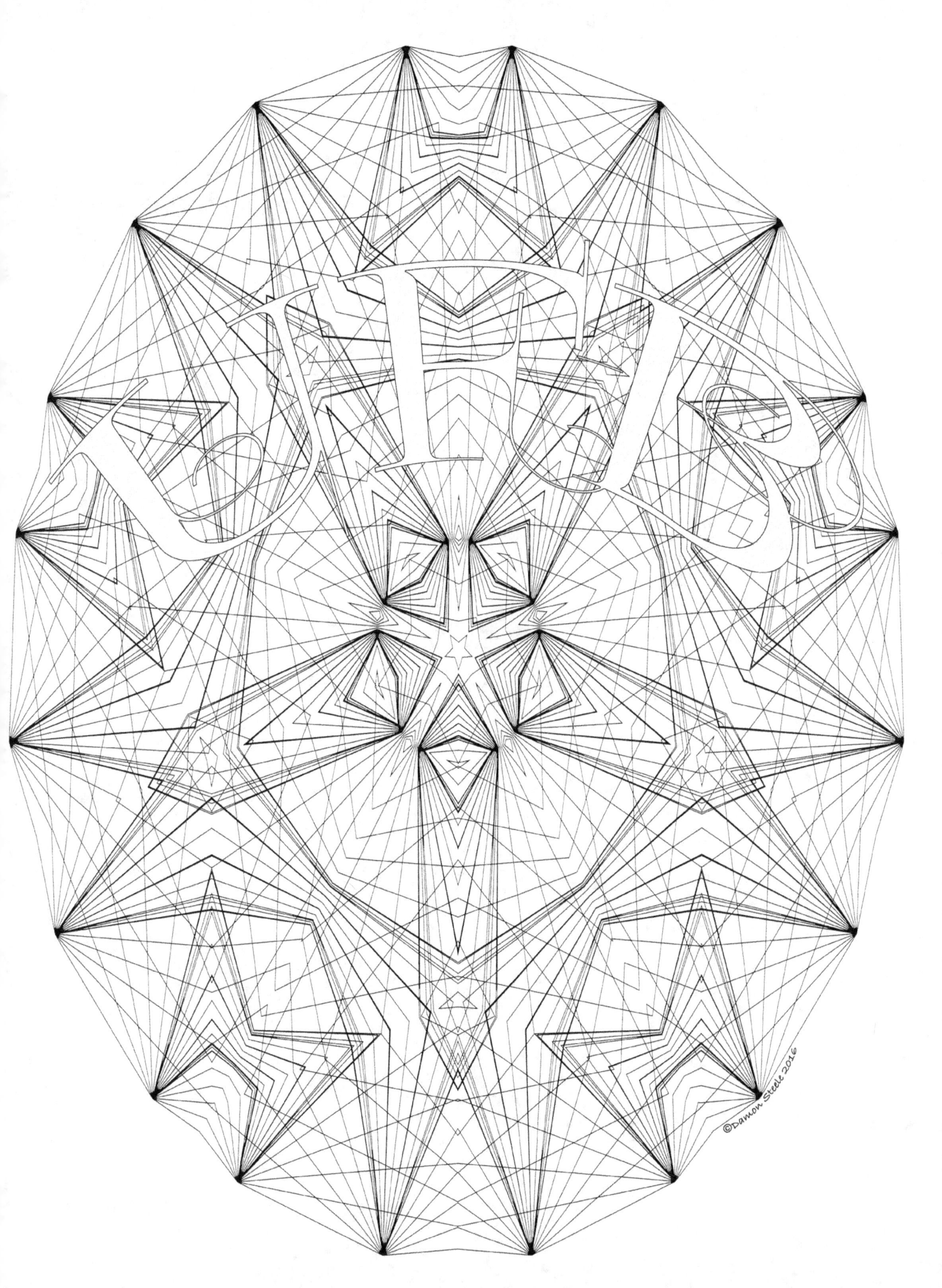

©Damon Steele 2016

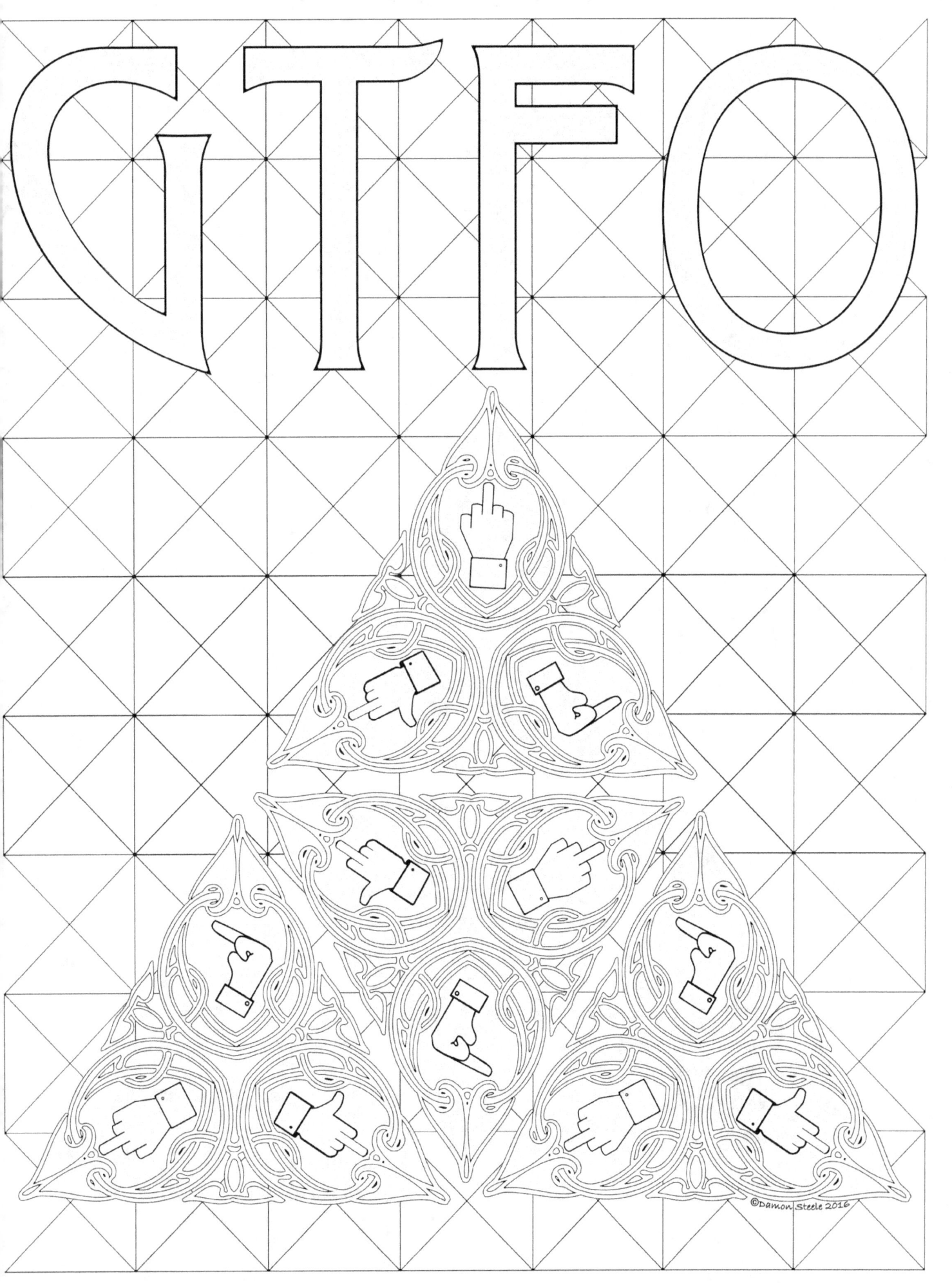